W9-BUM-652

RECEIVED
SEP 2 1 2006
By

HAYNER PUBLIC LIBRARY DISTRICT
ALTON, ILLINOIS

OVERDUES .10 PER DAY MAXIMUM FINE
COST OF BOOKS. LOST OR DAMAGED
BOOKS ADDITIONAL $5.00 SERVICE CHARGE.

BRANCH

ASTHMA

HAYNER PUBLIC LIBRARY DISTRICT
ALTON, ILLINOIS

ASTHMA

Ruth Bjorklund

BENCHMARK BOOKS

MARSHALL CAVENDISH
NEW YORK

HAYNER PUBLIC LIBRARY DISTRICT
ALTON, ILLINOIS

Special thanks to Miles Freeborn, Marijo Ratcliffe, and Dr. Paula Holmes-Eber

Marshall Cavendish Benchmark
99 White Plains Road
Tarrytown, New York 10591-9001
www.marshallcavendish.us

Text copyright © 2005 by Marshall Cavendish Corporation

All rights reserved. No part of this book may be reproduced or utilized in any form or by any means electronic or mechanical including photocopying, recording, or by any information storage and retrieval system, without permission from the copyright holders.

This book is not intended for use as a substitute for advice, consultation, or treatment by a licensed medical practitioner. The reader is advised that no action of a medical nature should be taken without consultation with a licensed medical practitioner, including action that may seem to be indicated by the contents of this work, since individual circumstances vary and medical standards, knowledge, and practices change with time. The publisher, author, and medical consultants disclaim all liability and cannot be held responsible for any problems that may arise from use of this book.

Library of Congress Cataloging-in-Publication Data

Bjorklund, Ruth.
    Asthma / by Ruth Bjorklund.
        p. cm. -- (Health alert)
    Includes bibliographical references and index.
    ISBN 0-7614-1803-2
    1. Asthma--Juvenile literature. I. Title. II. Series: Health alert (Benchmark Books)

    RC591.B54 2005
    616.2'38--dc22   2004005976

Front cover: An asthma inhaler
Title page: Allergens

Photo research by Regina Flanagan

Front cover: DigitalVision / Picture Quest
The photographs in this book are used by permission and through the courtesy of: *Photo Researchers, Inc.*: Carlyn Iverson, 9; Innerspace Imaging, 10; Medical Art Service, 11; Stem Jems, 12; Sophie Jacopin, 15; Eddy Gray, 2, 17; SciMAT, 19; Andrew Syred, 20; Mark Clarke, 23, 44, 52; SPL, 25; CC Studio, 26; Geoff Tompkinson, 30, 33; Jamse King-Holmes, 31; Burger, 36; Carolyn A. McKeone, 43; Damien Lovegrove, 46; Coneyl Jay, 50. *Corbis*: Bill Ross, 21; Bettmann, 27, 29; Austrian Archives, 28; Wolfgang Kaehler, 38; Reuters, 41; Micheal Keller, 42; Tim Mosenfelder, 53 (right); Duomo, 53 (center), Sunset Boulevard, 53 (right).

Printed in China
6 5 4 3 2

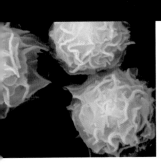

CONTENTS

WHAT IS IT LIKE TO HAVE ASTHMA?

Miles, a thirteen year old boy, can still clearly remember the night, ten years ago, when he woke up and could not breathe. "I felt something heavy on my chest and I remember trying to push it off. I couldn't inhale or exhale. It was so scary, I felt like I was in shock. I panicked. Now I know that when you get that worried, it makes it worse." The "it" Miles describes is his disease, asthma. That night, Miles was brought to the hospital for treatment.

After that night, life changed for Miles and his family. The doctors said that Miles' allergies had set off his asthma. Allergies are a negative reaction that the body has in response to substances called **allergens**. Some common allergens are mold, pollen, air pollution, cigarette smoke, and dust. When the family went home, they cleaned the house as best they could. But Miles never seemed to stay healthy for long. He caught frequent colds that often developed into painful pneumonia, which would then trigger the asthma. So while his sister, Ramona played outside, Miles often sat inside, breathing medicine through his **nebulizer** (a device that helps him breathe). They would later discover that because they lived in an area that was dark and damp, mold was growing underneath the carpets.

The family eventually moved to a different home. Though his health did improve, Miles was still left out of many activities that other children enjoyed. In the spring and fall when pollen counts were high, Miles' allergies would trigger bouts of asthma. Like many children with his disease, Miles has missed a lot of school. In fact, in the United States, all the children who have asthma together miss more than 14 million days of school each year. On the days Miles did attend school, he was no stranger to the nurse's office. During recess, he would lose energy running around. Frequently, he retreated to the swings to sit and watch the other kids play.

After one particularly bad year, Miles and his parents visited an allergy specialist to see if he had any allergies they did not already know about. The doctor gave Miles several allergy tests and his suggestions helped Miles and his family to better manage his disease. Armed with more knowledge about his asthma, his health improved. He even played on a roller hockey team.

Now that Miles is older, he takes more responsibility for caring for himself and his disease. "When I feel tired, and my chest starts to hurt, I just focus on trying to relax and breathe normally. I drink a lot of water and I take vitamins when there's lots of pollen. I know where my medicine is, if I need it. But I am not afraid to go outside and do things. I think that if I move around a lot, I'll be stronger for it." Miles plays the drums and he says that sometimes he gets so excited playing, that it triggers his asthma. "That's kind of embarrassing. I have to tell the band that I need to take a break and sit down. The same thing happens if I am walking somewhere with my friends. I lose energy and I just need to stop and rest. Sometimes they wait for me. And sometimes they say, 'Catch up!'" Miles grins, "That's just the way it goes, I guess!"

WHAT IS ASTHMA?

Asthma affects the lungs and a person's ability to breathe normally. It is the most common **chronic** disease among children in the United States. A chronic disease is one that does not ever go away. About 6 million American children have asthma and nearly 14 million adults do. Throughout the world, the number of asthma cases reported has doubled in the last three decades. There are more than 100 million people worldwide who are known to be suffering from the disease.

There is no cure for asthma, and it can be fatal if left untreated. Each year, more than 5,000 Americans die from untreated asthma. Outside of the United States, more than 35,000 people die each year from complications of the disease.

Researchers have found that people with asthma inherit a tendency, or likelihood, to develop asthma. Children whose parents have asthma have a 40 percent chance of developing the disease. Some asthmatics may not show any **symptoms** of the disease until later in life. Many children with asthma "grow out" of the disease, but asthma can always return.

To understand the disease, it is important to have a general idea of how the respiratory, circulatory, and immune systems work in a healthy body.

THE RESPIRATORY SYSTEM

The respiratory system is made up of organs used in breathing such as the nose, mouth, trachea, bronchi, and lungs. When a person breathes in, air enters the nose or mouth, and travels down the throat into a tube called the trachea. The trachea is also known as the windpipe. The trachea extends from the back of the throat down into the chest. There it divides into two branches, or airways, called **bronchi**. Each bronchi is called a bronchus. Each bronchus leads into one of the two lungs. Within the lungs, each

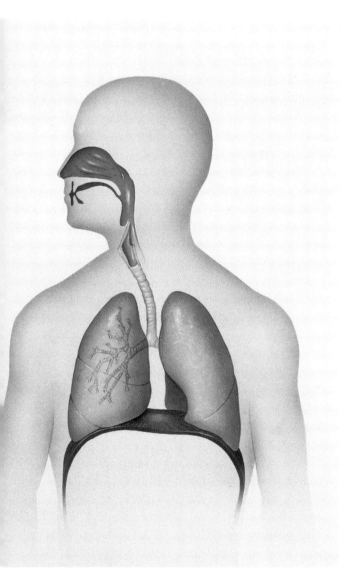

Asthma is a disease that affects a person's respiratory system, shown in this illustration.

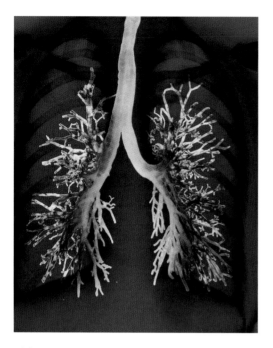

This colored chest X ray shows how the bronchi divide into many smaller bronchi and even smaller bronchioles.

bronchus divides into many smaller tubes called **bronchioles**. The bronchioles end in millions of tiny sacs called **alveoli**, which fill with incoming air. The tubes through which air flows during breathing are often called the airways.

Wrapped around the bronchi and the bronchioles are bands of bronchial muscle that control the flow of air through the tubes. When the bronchial muscles relax, the airways widen, allowing air to flow readily. When the bronchial muscles tighten, the airways become narrow, reducing or stopping the flow of air.

Inside the airways, a layer of cells produces a sticky liquid called **mucus**. Mucus keeps the inside walls of the airways moist. It also filters the incoming air by trapping dust and other irritating particles. Also lining the inside walls of the bronchi and bronchioles are slender hair-like structures known as cilia. Cilia whip back and forth to move the mucus up toward the throat. Many times a day, small amounts of mucus are swallowed, or at times, coughed or sneezed out. This gets rid of substances that were trapped in it, and prevents them from collecting in the lungs.

THE CIRCULATORY SYSTEM

The body's circulatory system, or bloodstream, delivers blood all through the body. The heart pumps the blood through millions of tubes called blood vessels. The blood is constantly moving through the vessels because of the heart's pumping action. Some of the blood vessels carry blood to the lungs. In the lungs, the air-filled alveoli are surrounded by tiny blood vessels called capillaries. Blood that is moving through the capillaries picks up oxygen from the air in the alveoli. The capillaries then carry the oxygenated blood into larger blood vessels that lead out of the lungs and back to the heart. Once in the heart, the oxygenated blood is pumped through-out the body.

As cells of the body use the oxygen, they produce a waste gas called carbon dioxide. The carbon dioxide leaves the cells and collects in the bloodstream. Blood carries the carbon dioxide to the lungs and into the

During respiration, oxygen and carbon dioxide are exchanged in the alveoli. Many blood vessels run through and around the alveoli.

capillaries that surround the alveoli. The carbon dioxide then moves out of the blood into the air in the alveoli. When a person exhales, carbon dioxide is pushed out through the airways and expelled through the mouth or nose. The blood vessels that are involved in carrying blood to and from the lungs are called the pulmonary vessels, or sometimes the pulmonary circuit. The word pulmonary refers to the lungs.

THE IMMUNE SYSTEM

The immune system is made up of many cells, chemicals, and organs that work together to fight off foreign substances that enter the body. These substances include dust, germs, bacteria, and viruses. White blood cells, also called **lymphocytes**, are an important part of the immune system and travel throughout the bloodstream to defend the body from invading substances. Some white blood cells, called B-cells, identify harmful invaders and flag them

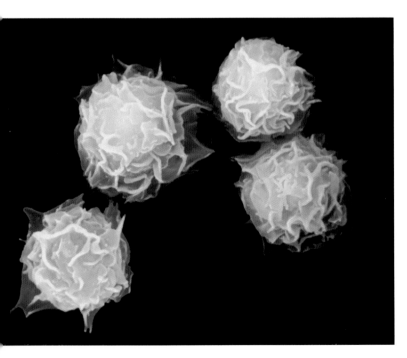

A microscopic look at mast cells.

with a chemical known as an **antibody.** Other white blood cells, called phagocytes (Greek for "eating cells") surround and digest the flagged invaders. Some of the B-cells are able to make antibodies long after the invader has been cleared from the body. Those cells are called memory cells. The next time the same type of invader enters the body, the memory cells make antibodies immediately. This helps the immune system recognize and destroy the harmful foreign substance even faster than before.

T-cells are another important type of white blood cell. There are several varieties of T-cells. Some circulate in the body and release **toxic** (deadly) chemicals that destroy invaders like the cold virus. A different group of T-cells direct the activities of the many different types of immune system cells as they identify and attack harmful substances in the body.

Another type of immune system cell is the **mast cell.** These cells are found in many areas of the body, including the respiratory system, where they can be found in the walls of the airways. When connected to certain antibodies, called **immunoglobulin E** or **IgE,** the mast cells release strong chemicals to fight off invaders. **Histamine** is one of these mast cell chemicals. In addition to helping fight off invaders, histamine causes the bronchial muscles in the airways to contract or tighten. Mast cell chemicals also cause the airways to become swollen and watery. This swollen and watery condition, called inflammation, allows the white blood cells to move about more freely while attacking the invader.

When a healthy body fights a cold virus, histamine and the

other mast cells chemicals are produced, causing inflammation of the airways. A person with a cold will cough, sneeze, sniffle, and have teary eyes. These symptoms are a sign that the body is fighting off the invading cold virus. Inflammation of the airways can also happen when a person inhales pollen, dust, harsh chemicals, tobacco smoke, and many other substances.

TAKING A BREATH

Inside the chest and along the bottom of the lungs is the diaphragm, a sheet of muscle that regulates breathing. The diaphragm can change shape from being flat to being a little dome-shaped. When a person breathes in, the diaphragm flattens. That causes the chest area to enlarge, pulling fresh air into the lungs. When the diaphragm relaxes it becomes dome-shaped, causing the chest area to get smaller. That pushes used air out of the lungs.

When a healthy person breathes in, oxygen-rich air flows through the airways and into the alveoli of the lungs. Dust and other particles are captured by the mucus, which acts like a filter. Bronchial muscles squeeze and relax around the airways to control the passage of the filtered air into the alveoli. Oxygen is delivered to the blood in the capillaries, and carbon dioxide is removed from the blood. As the person exhales, air in the alveoli is pushed out, carrying the carbon dioxide away. A healthy young person performs this task of breathing, without thinking, sixteen to twenty-two times a minute, each minute of the day.

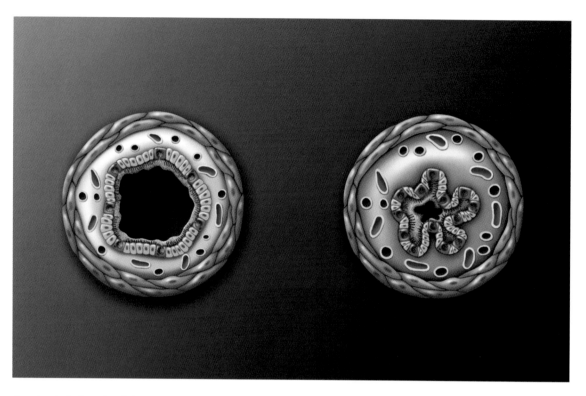

On the left is a healthy, open bronchiole. The narrowed bronchiole on the right has been affected by asthma and air cannot freely pass through it.

But a person with asthma can suddenly have trouble breathing. This is called an asthma attack, or an asthma **episode**, flare, or flare up. An asthma attack is a series of events that is uncomfortable and can be very serious. Something known as an asthma **trigger** sparks an episode by causing the immune system cells to overreact. As a result, the person's airways become inflamed. The airways of a person with asthma are always somewhat swollen and inflamed, and the airways' reaction to a trigger makes the inflammation worse. The mucus-making cells overreact by producing too much mucus. The mucus clogs the bronchi and the bronchioles, and the cilia are unable to push it up and out. At the same time, mast cells release their chemicals. These chemicals make the bronchial muscles contract, squeezing the airways until the air passages are nearly blocked. This nearly reduces the flow of air in and out of the alveoli. Carbon dioxide wastes build up and cannot be exhaled.

A person suffering from an asthma attack feels a tightening in the chest and will cough and gasp for air. While the bronchial muscles are contracted, air squeezes through the narrowed passages in the airways. The air makes a whistling sound, called **wheezing**. The episode can be over quickly, or it can last for several hours, if a person does not use his or her medication. In extreme cases, a person may need to go to a hospital for emergency care.

Once an episode ends, the airways and lungs do return to normal. Sometimes it can take several days or weeks before they do so. The whole process begins again the next time a person with asthma is exposed to an asthma trigger.

ASTHMA TRIGGERS

Triggers are the substances or circumstances that cause an asthma attack. Many people with asthma react to more than one trigger. Some common triggers are viral infections, allergens, environmental irritants, weather, emotions, and exercise.

There are more than two hundred different viruses that can cause colds, influenza (the flu), and sinus infections. These viruses are often very contagious. Children in school are likely to catch

An electron micrograph shows inhaled allergens such as pollen and dust stuck on the walls of the trachea.

four to eight colds a year. When a person with asthma catches a cold, the immune system often overreacts, causing an asthma episode. "Some winters we have terrible viruses," says a hospital nurse, "and even people with mild cases of asthma who regularly take good care of themselves can get sick and land in the hospital."

The most frequent triggers for people with asthma is exposure to an allergen. An allergen is something a person comes into contact with that triggers inflammation. A person is said to be allergic to something if his or her body reacts to it by breathing, touching, smelling, or eating it. When a person with allergies breathes in an allergen, his or her immune system considers it an enemy, and takes action against it. IgE antibodies develop to fight the invader. Mast cells rally to secrete their chemicals. The person's airways swell, thicken with mucus, and become constricted by bronchial muscle spasms.

Many people have allergies, but not all people with allergies have asthma. Each time a person with asthma undergoes an allergic reaction, he or she becomes even more allergic to the allergen, making the symptoms worse the next time. "It's a vicious cycle," says one nurse. People with asthma can be allergic to foods such as peanuts, tree nuts (cashews, walnuts, pecans), fish, wheat, soy, eggs, and milk products. Still others develop allergies from prolonged exposure to something in their workplace. Carpenters can become allergic to sawdust and health care workers can develop allergies to the latex gloves they wear.

In spring and fall, when plants reproduce and send out **pollen**, "hay fever" season begins, and people with pollen allergies suffer. Also during these periods, farmers and gardeners churn up wet soil and leaves, exposing people to molds, another common allergen. Molds also grow in damp areas inside people's homes: in houseplants, basements, around leaky windows and pipes, and under carpeting.

Other unwelcome household allergens are due to pests, such as dust mites and cockroaches. Dust mites are harmless, microscopic, spiderlike creatures that live anywhere there is dust. They feed on the dust that collects in places like rugs, blankets, pillows, closets, furniture, and bookshelves. Cockroaches are hard-shelled insects that live in warm climates, but also indoors in colder areas, especially in poorly maintained older buildings. They feed on scraps of food. It is not actually the insects themselves, but their dried up feces (excreted waste material) that generate a strong reaction in people with pest allergies.

Animals with fur or feathers also create allergens. Flaked-off skin from furred animals is called **dander**. Many people are allergic to the pet dander produced by cats, dogs, hamsters, or horses. The feathers of a pet bird can also cause allergic reactions.

Some medicines can cause asthma episodes. Aspirin and

What's in Your Dust?

The dust that collects in your house comes from many different things. In a single gram of house dust, you might find food crumbs, salt and sugar crystals, synthetic (manmade) fibers, natural fibers (wool, cotton, paper, and silk), pollen, flakes of human skin, human hair, fingernail filings, animal fur, flakes of animal skin, dried saliva and urine from pets, glass particles, glue, insect parts, oil, soot, ash, paint chips, plant particles, soil, spores, fungi, stone particles, and wood shavings. Many of these things can be allergens so it is important to try to keep your environment clean and dust free.

A microscopic view of household dust shows pollen grains, fungal spores, skin flakes, plant fragments, cotton fibers, and hair particles.

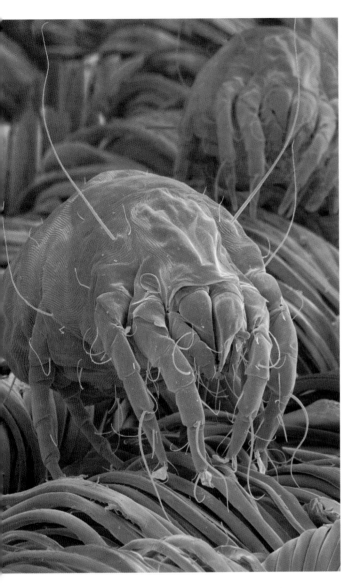
These dust mites are living on fabric fibers. The mites are far too small for the naked eye to see.

ibuprofen are examples. These are used for headaches or other pain, but people with asthma can take acetaminophen as a painkiller instead.

Clean air is vital to a person with asthma. Outside, air pollution from industrial factories and refineries, exhaust from cars and trucks, and smoke and ash from fireplaces and woodstoves can provoke an asthma attack. City dwellers with asthma have to be extremely careful when dangerous chemicals from car exhaust, factories, and fuel-burning power plants mix with sunlight. When these chemicals combine with sunlight, they create a form of air pollution known as ground-level ozone, or **smog**. Children are especially harmed by smog, because their lungs are smaller and because children are more likely to be

Smog collects over Los Angeles. Asthma sufferers should be careful about being outside during periods of heavy smog.

outside playing in summer, when smog usually is at its worst. Indoor air pollutants are also especially harmful to people with asthma. Some of the most offensive triggers are strong fumes from household cleansers, paint, solvents, perfume, scented soaps, and cooking odors. By far, the worst indoor pollutant is tobacco smoke.

Some people with asthma are sensitive to certain weather conditions. Cold or very dry air can bring on an asthma attack.

Also, a sudden change in temperature can cause an attack. A person with asthma can suffer an attack simply by leaving a hot, sunny patio and entering a chilly, air-conditioned room. Changes in air pressure (barometric pressure) can also play a part. Sometimes an electrical storm can trigger an asthma attack.

Emotions can also be a trigger for a person with asthma. Laughing, crying, or being angry can cause a person with asthma to breathe rapidly. This rapid breathing can irritate the lungs and cause an asthma episode.

A painful asthma trigger is acid reflux, known medically as gastroesophageal reflux. When a person swallows food, acids in the stomach are ready to digest it. Sometimes, especially in babies, the stomach acid sloshes back up and goes into the lungs. The lungs become irritated, and in a person with asthma, this irritation can lead to an attack.

Exercise is a common non-allergy trigger for people with asthma. In many individuals, it may be their only asthma trigger. During exercise, the body uses up more oxygen, and a person will breathe harder and faster to deliver more oxygen to muscles. When this takes place, breathing happens so quickly that the nose is unable to warm and moisten the air. This makes the lungs cold, dry, and irritated.

Clearly, a wide range of triggers can provoke asthma symptoms. While certain triggers may cause an asthma flare in one person, they may not have any affect on another person. For some people, it can take three or more triggers before an asthma episode gets underway.

Asthma takes many forms. For some, it is mild, and symptoms can be fairly easy to control. But for others, it can be severe, calling for constant watchfulness. All people with asthma need to learn everything they can about their disease and know what triggers their symptoms. Once they know more, they can do things to control their environment and take the proper medication.

Asthma patients should ask their doctors to recommend what amount and type of physical activity is best for them. Many people with asthma who play sports keep medicine handy in case they have a flare-up.

3

THE HISTORY OF ASTHMA

Doctors today are able to treat asthma patients because of the knowledge gained from thousands of years of research. For more than four thousand years, medical experts have recognized the disease we now know as asthma. Around 2600 B.C.E. a Chinese medical scholar known as the Yellow Emperor wrote an important medical book that included a description of the disease. The scholar recommended acupuncture as a treatment. This involved inserting long, thin needles through the skin into selected acupuncture sites of the body. There are more than 350 sites, and peope believe that inserting needles into sites that relate to the lungs could increase the flow of energy and improve their health. The Chinese scholar also advised asthma sufferers to eat parts of a plant called *ma huang*. This plant contains a chemical that is sometimes used today to treat asthma.

Hippocrates was a well-known doctor who lived in ancient Greece sometime between 460 and 380 B.C.E. Some say that Hippocrates was the first to name the disease. In his writings, he described patients with troubled breathing. The word he used, *asthma* comes from a Greek verb that means "to pant."

Other ancient Greek, Egyptian, and Roman medical scholars treated the disease and wrote about its symptoms. Galen of Pergamum was a physician who lived in Rome around 157 C.E. He believed that asthma sufferers were having problems with their bronchial tubes and lungs.

During the Dark Ages (around the 400s to the 900s C.E.), a doctor in service to an Egyptian ruler tended

Galien natif de Pergame ville d'Asie, excellent Medecin viuoit du temps des Empereurs Antonin le Philosophe et de Commodus, on tient qu'il a vescu 140 ans.

An illustration of the respected physician Galen of Pergamum.

the ruler's asthmatic son. The doctor, Moses Maimonides, suggested remedies that included less stress, a dry climate, and chicken soup. Maimonides also believed that each person with asthma needed to be treated according to his or her own individual needs.

Though many of these doctors had some good ideas, it was not until the 1600s that researchers recognized some of the causes of asthma, such as heredity, air quality, weather, and exercise. Around the 1660s the English physician Thomas Sydenham determined that asthma was a lung problem associated with clogged bronchial tubes.

NEW INVENTIONS AND NEW TREATMENTS

Asthma research progressed even further in the 1800s. The invention of the stethoscope helped a great deal. By using the stethoscope, doctors could listen to the sounds of air moving through an asthma patient's airways. Early stethoscopes were much simpler than the ones used by doctors today, but they helped doctors gain more information about their ill patients. A helpful instrument called a **spirometer** was developed. This instrument measures the volume of air the lungs can hold, and the force with which the air as it is exhaled. Spirometers are still used today. By the 1860s, doctors knew that asthma could be

Like modern-day stethoscopes, the early forms of this instrument were placed against a patient's chest. A doctor put his or her ear to the other end to hear a patient's heartbeat and breaths.

triggered by strong smells and particles in the air such as animal dander or plant material.

Though doctors continued to better understand asthma, many of their methods of healing were less than desirable. Most of them thought smoking tobacco would relieve the symptoms. People now know that smoking tobacco is one of the worst things a person with asthma can do. Asthmatics in America were told to go to different places where the air was cleaner and drier. Many moved to the western and southwestern They stayed at spas and other retreats that were supposed to help people with medical conditions. People suffering from asthma also bought the special healing tonics and powders that were advertised in newspapers across the country. These "medicines" were supposed to cure many different illnesses, including asthma.

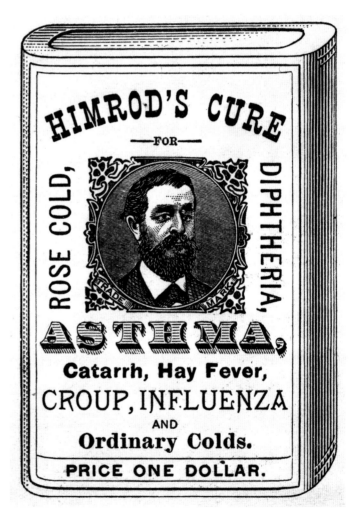

HIMROD'S CURE
—FOR—
ROSE COLD, DIPHTHERIA,
ASTHMA,
Catarrh, Hay Fever,
CROUP, INFLUENZA
AND
Ordinary Colds.
PRICE ONE DOLLAR.

In the 1800s and early 1900s, many "medicine doctors" claimed their special tonics could cure several illnesses, including asthma.

These asthma patients who lived in Germany in the 1930s use special masks to help them breathe.

Usually these tonics were nothing more than flavored syrups. Often the mixtures were made from chemicals that did more harm than good.

In 1903 scientists were able to determine that a human hormone called adrenaline could help asthma patients. By the 1920s doctors were treating asthma with ephedrine. This medicine was derived from the *ma huang* plant that ancient Chinese doctors had used to treat asthma. While drugs such as these helped, some doctors still prescribed dangerous treatments that did not help. For example in the 1940s, researchers at an asthma center for children believed that children suffered asthma because of their parents. The cure was a parentectomy, in which children were taken from their families to live at the center, away from the stress of family

In the 1960s, research centers such as the National Jewish Hospital at Denver helped many children with asthma. These boys are exercising their lungs through blowing games.

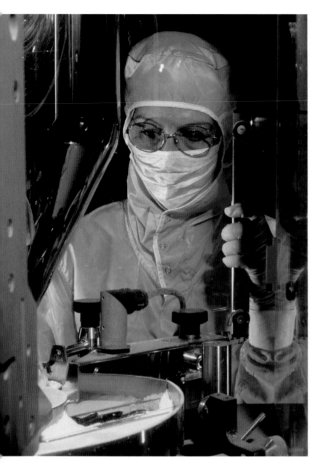

New discoveries in asthma medication help millions of asthma patients each year.

life. Other physicians thought that asthma could be cured by sleeping upside down.

In the 1960s doctors discovered that asthma attacks were linked to allergic reactions. Allergy research helped to further asthma research. Cortisone drugs were developed based on natural chemicals found in the body. These drugs reduced inflammation. Scientists were able to produce cortisone drugs that could be used to ease inflammation in the bronchial tubes and lungs. By the 1970s cortisone inhalers became available to the public. These helped a patient inhale the medicine so that it could go directly into the respiratory system. Since then, scientists have continued to improve inhalers and the medicines inside them.

In the 1990s doctors realized that most people with asthma had lungs that were always somewhat swollen and inflamed. This led them to understand that someone with a serious case of asthma should have medicine every day, and not just when an asthma episode occured. Today, the immune system is a major area of study for asthma researchers. Many think that a malfunction of the immune system is responsible for asthma attacks. Progress in genetic research has also helped. Scientists are trying to identify the **gene** or genes that are linked to asthma. They hope to some-day be able to alter a person's genetic material so that he or she will not develop asthma.

Advances in understanding and treating asthma are happening all the time. People who had childhood asthma forty years ago are now healthier than they were then, thanks to new discoveries and new medicines. Nevertheless, asthma continues to be serious problem and more knowledge is needed, so researchers continue to find ways to help people with asthma.

By studying the human immune system, scientists hope to find ways to help people who suffer from allergies and asthma.

4

LIVING WITH ASTHMA

Although asthma is not a disease that can be cured, with proper care, asthmatics can live normal, productive lives. Each case of asthma should be treated individually, because the triggers that aggravate symptoms vary from person to person.

The best possible first step toward a healthy, active life is visiting a medical clinician such as a family doctor, asthma specialist, or pulmonary care practitioner. This visit has two major parts, a physical examination and a study of the patient's past asthma episodes. A doctor performs a physical examination to check the patient's breathing and to listen to air moving in and out of the patient's airways. The examination often includes a chest X ray. An X ray can show an obstruction in the airways, but that usually is visible only if the patient is having difficulty breathing at the time. In more severe cases of asthma, an X ray may show evidence of trapped air in the lungs or other signs of breathing complications.

As the testing continues, a **pulmonary function test**, or PFT is performed. The patient breathes into a mouthpiece connected to a

A medical specialist monitors an asthma patient's lung function using computerized technology.

spirometer, which records the volume of air breathed in and out. After the PFT, the doctor reviews the results and will likely be able to determine if the patient has asthma, and if so, how serious it is.

If the doctor determines that the patient has asthma, then the doctor and patient need to explore together the triggers that irritate the lungs and cause asthma symptoms to flare. The first

Many symptoms of other respiratory illnesses resemble those of asthma, like a runny nose, watery eyes, wheezing, coughing, shortness of breath, and loss of energy. Most asthma experts will say that it is impossible to truly **diagnose** asthma in someone younger than six years old. Up to that age, a person with asthma-like symptoms will be diagnosed as having reactive airway disease, or RAD, instead. Some of the medicines used to treat RAD are also used to treat asthma, but some are not. Doctors watch to see if a child has asthma symptoms over a period of time such as five or six years. Frequently, an infant can seem to have asthma, only to have it disappear after two or three years.

step is to see whether allergies trigger asthma episodes. A visit to an allergy specialist, or allergist, for an exam is the best course to take. An allergist will look for relationships between allergens in the patient's environment and asthma flares. Sometimes the allergist will test a patient's reaction to different allergens.

Allergies can be treated with medicine. By treating their allergies, many asthmatics are better able to control their asthma episodes. Allergy medicines come in pills or as a liquid that a person sprays into his or her nose. Every so often, an allergy specialist will recommend immunotherapy, or allergy shots. The allergist will give the patient increasing doses of allergens over periods of time, to help the immune system become less sensitive to the allergen.

To provide the best possible asthma treatment, a doctor must not only decide what the triggers are, but also the severity of a patient's asthma. Asthma has four levels of severity. They are called mild intermittent, mild persistent, moderate persistent, and severe persistent. Intermittent means every once in awhile, persistent means constant. The levels are based on how often and how severe asthma attacks are when a patient is not using asthma medicines.

People are said to have mild intermittent asthma if they have fewer than two wheezing episodes per week and generally have only one or two triggers that bring on an asthma flare. They can often go for long stretches of time without any flares at all. People have mild persistent asthma if they have slightly more than two wheezing episodes per week, and slightly more than two flares during the night each month. The people with either type of mild asthma have lungs that function with at least 80 percent of their ability all of the time. People with mild intermittent asthma take medications only during a flare, while people with mild persistent asthma should take some daily medication, as well as medication whenever an episode occurs.

People with moderate persistent asthma have daily symptoms, frequent bouts of wheezing during the week, and at least one nighttime flare per week. Their lungs function between 60 and 80 percent of normal and they must take regular medications daily to control their symptoms. A small minority of people with asthma has a severe persistent level of the disease. These patients have constant symptoms, daily asthma flares, and must make quite an effort to breathe because their lungs function below 60 percent of their capacity. Persons with severe persistent asthma require large doses of medications and must often refrain from excess activity.

After the diagnosis is made and treatment begins, people with asthma see their symptoms improve. "The good thing about asthma

Asthma attacks can occur at different times of the day—even at night while a person is trying to sleep.

is that it can be managed," reports asthma educator Marijo Ratcliffe. Getting enough sleep, drinking plenty of water, exercising, and eating healthy foods are other ways to stay healthy naturally. If a person has asthma, the healthier they are, the less often they will experience asthma symptoms. There are many ways to manage and treat the disease and new and improved medicines are being developed.

TRIGGER PREVENTION

The first major step to controlling asthma is to know what it is that triggers a reaction. Friends and family can help the patient recognize his or her triggers. Health care providers have numerous checklists, questionnaires, and tests that can help make sense of what the triggers might be. Once the triggers are known, then the task of dealing with them begins.

The first step to controlling asthma is to avoid the triggers.

Many people discover that their family's pet is a trigger. The pet should stay outside as much as possible. Family members should keep the pet off the furniture and out of the bedroom of the person with asthma. If the reaction to the pet is severe, the family should find the pet a new home. If colds and flu are triggers, then precautions such as keeping away from people who are sick, getting a flu shot, and washing hands frequently can make a difference. If cold winter weather provokes asthma flares, then wearing a scarf or ski mask over the mouth and nose and breathing through the fabric will warm the air and lessen irritation to the lungs.

Other outdoor triggers such as air pollution, smog, or pollen are hard to avoid. Many weather reports and Web sites give pollen counts to help people with allergies know how much and what kind of pollen is in the air each day. Different plants release their pollen at different times of the year. It is important to make note of which pollens are the most bothersome and when they are in the air. For many people, the most irritating pollens are from ragweed grass, and from birch and oak trees. Midday is the time when pollen counts are normally at their lowest, so if a person with asthma needs to be outside, that is the best time. After being in pollen-rich air, a person with asthma should be sure to shampoo before going to bed, so that pollen trapped in hair does not rub off on bedding and irritate the lungs at night. Asthma sufferers with serious allergies to pollen or other airborne allergens should stay indoors and keep the windows closed. When traveling in a car, windows should also remain closed, with the air-conditioner on.

On windy days throughout different times of the year, high levels of tree and flower pollen are in the air.

If strong smells such as soap, hairspray, or perfume are triggers, then a person with asthma should be comfortable asking friends and family to use something unscented. It is also very important for a person with asthma to be comfortable asking someone to stop smoking tobacco nearby. If that is impossible, the person with asthma should leave the room. The carbon dioxide that escapes from tobacco smoke is very damaging to everyone's lungs, especially those with hypersensitive airways.

Many people with asthma react to the feces of cockroaches and dust mites. Cockroaches are often associated with old buildings that are falling apart, but cockroaches can be found in any home located in warm, damp climates. To prevent the bugs from coming in, all leaks and cracks in walls, windows and plumbing should be sealed. Food should not be left out to attract insects. Using a dehumidifier will reduce the dampness that cockroaches like. Dust mites exist everywhere, even in the most spotless homes. A person with asthma should avoid things in the house that trap dust, like soft upholstered furniture, carpeting, or heavy curtains. Tile, linoleum, or hardwood floors with washable area rugs are easiest to keep clean and dust-free. Closets, bookcases, and window blinds are notorious dust collectors and require frequent cleaning. Many people with asthma store very few items in their rooms and some remove closet doors so that there are no forgotten corners where dust can collect. Keeping clutter to a minimum and dusting with a damp cloth also prevents the dust from becoming airborne.

Vacuuming regularly with a special micro-filter called HEPA (high efficiency particulate arrestor) is extremely important. Regular vacuum cleaners can blow dust around and put even more into the air. Ideally, people with asthma should not be in the room during dusting and vacuuming, but when they are, they should wear a dust mask. Every two weeks all sheets, blankets, pillowcases, and stuffed animals should be washed in hot water (around 130 degrees

Fahrenheit). Mattresses, box springs, and pillows should be covered in plastic or special allergen-proof zippered bags that keep dust from passing through them. Some say it is a good idea to seal over the zippers with duct tape. Bedding made of synthetic fibers is best, because it holds less dust and debris than bedding made of natural materials, such as feathers, cotton, and wool.

Molds are a common allergen found both indoors and outdoors. Molds thrive in damp places such as basements, bathrooms, kitchens, or in the soil of houseplants. Limiting houseplants, repairing leaky faucets, scrubbing damp areas with water and bleach, and keeping the house drier by using a dehumidifier can help. Many of the strategies used to tackle pollen and dust mites also help reduce exposure to molds. Raking leaves is not a good chore for a person with hypersensitivity to molds. And on windy days, a person with mold allergies and asthma is better off staying indoors.

Some people have exercise-induced asthma. This is one trigger that should *not* be avoided. In the past, people with asthma believed they needed to stay calm and avoid strenuous activity. But exercise is important to everyone's health. United States President Theodore Roosevelt had asthma but was still a rugged outdoorsman. He was as active as his lungs would allow, and his activity strengthened him and increased his lung capacity.

Asthmatics today can enjoy nearly any sport they choose, especially if they take medication beforehand. People with exercise-induced asthma should warm up before, and cool down after, vigorous exercise. They should also avoid being outside when air pollution or pollen levels are high, or when it is very cold, or very dry. If they feel a need to rest, they should. But none of these safety measures should hinder a person from playing hard at sports.

TAKING MEDICINE

As any person with asthma will tell you, there is more to coping with the disease than avoiding triggers. Some triggers cannot be avoided, and sometimes even if they are, people still get sick. Modern asthma medicines play a huge role in the well being of a person with asthma.

Although some asthma medicines come in pills or

Having asthma did not prevent Jackie Joyner-Kersee from competing in the Olympics.

syrups, most are taken with the aid of an inhaler. An inhaler is an L-shaped plastic tube that has a mouthpiece and a canister of medicine. Sometimes called a puffer or an MDI (metered dose inhaler), it is very portable. A person taking medicine with an inhaler puts his or her lips over the mouthpiece and presses down on the canister to release a spray of medicine at the right dose. At the same time, the person takes a slow, careful, deep breath. To insure that the medicine gets deep into the lungs, a spacer can be added to the inhaler. As the canister is pressed, the medicine

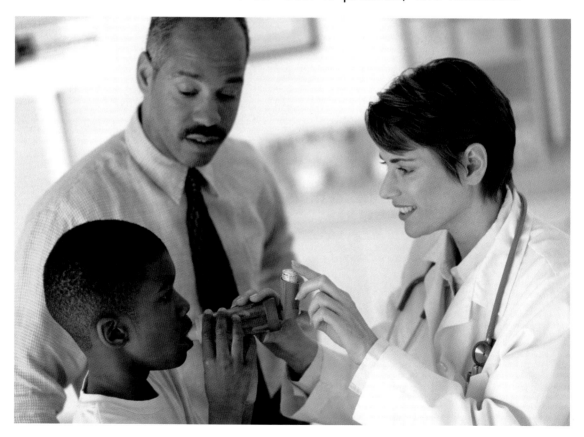

A doctor shows an asthma patient how to use his inhaler properly.

enters the spacer chamber instead of directly into the person's mouth. This allows the person to breathe in at a more measured and calm pace, and makes certain that none of the medicine is lost. Drug companies are making new inhaled medications called DPIs, or dry powder inhalers. These inhalers contain a very fine powder that patients breathe in. The powdered medicine in a DPI does not taste quite as bad as the medicine in mist inhalers does. Washing the face and rinsing out the mouth is recommended after taking all asthma medicines.

Many young people need an adult's help when using an inhaler.

Sometimes a person with asthma is too sick or too young to use an inhaler, even with the spacer. In these instances, a nebulizer is used. A nebulizer works somewhat like an inhaler, but it is attached to an air compressor and must be plugged in. A nebulizer works by mixing asthma medicine with a sterile saline solution to create a very fine mist that the patient breathes in. A person can even be sleeping while breathing in medicine from a nebulizer. A breathing mask attached to a nebulizer makes

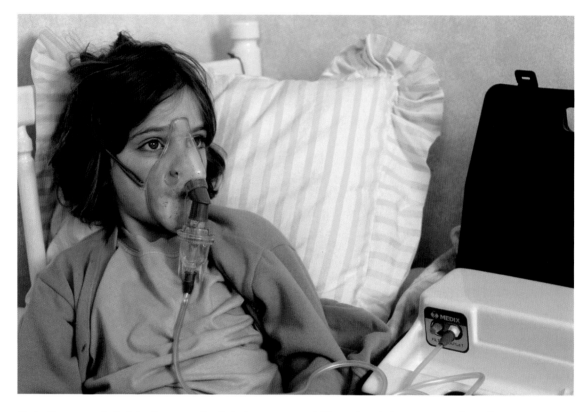

Nebulizers are helpful when regular inhalers cannot deliver the right amount of medicine.

it easier to use. Some people need a nebulizer only once in a while, so they rent them from pharmacies or medical supply houses. Other people use it more frequently, and decide to buy one. If the person travels a lot, purchasing a nebulizer with a battery-powered air compressor is a convenient choice, because it does not need to be plugged in.

RESCUE AND CONTROLLER MEDICINES

There are two general kinds of asthma medicines, rescue (or emergency) medicine, which is only taken during an asthma flare, and controller (or maintenance) medicine that is taken daily, to prevent asthma flares.

The most common rescue medicines are called **beta-agonists**, or more commonly, **bronchodilators**. Bronchodilators dilate, or open up, the airways by relaxing the bronchial muscles that surround them. One of the most common bronchodilators is called albuterol. Albuterol and similar drugs work quickly, within five to fifteen minutes and are usually taken at the start of an asthma attack. This medicine's effects last for four to six hours. Another bronchodilator is ipatropium bromide. It does not act as fast, but many doctors believe that it also helps reduce the amount of mucus in the lungs.

Corticosteroids are another type of rescue medicine. These medicines, like prednisone, relieve the painful swelling that obstructs the airways. Corticosteroids are hormones made naturally by the body's adrenal glands. There also are manmade versions, which are powerful antiinflammatory medicines. Corticosteroids are taken either as a pill or syrup when a patient has a serious asthma flare. Corticosteroids are sometimes just called steroids, but they should not be confused with anabolic steroids that some people take to build muscle.

Controller medicines are taken daily to lessen symptoms and prevent asthma episodes from occurring. Corticosteroids taken as a mist from an inhaler prevent inflammation in the airways of the lungs. Because this medicine is inhaled directly into the lungs, it is very effective and safe. Long-acting bronchodilators are another kind of controller medicine that are inhaled daily and directly into

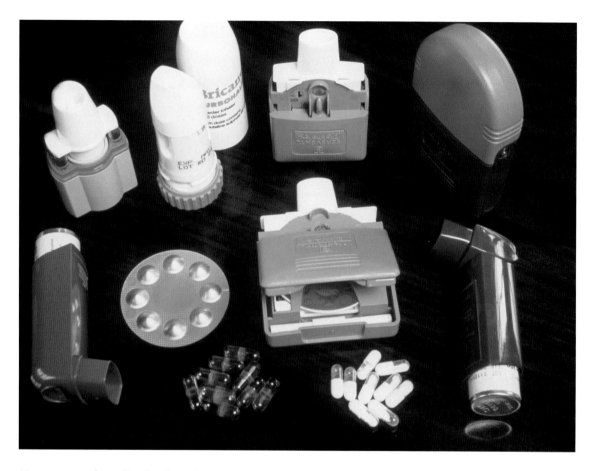

Many types of medication have been developed to help people who suffer from different levels of asthma.

the lungs to keep bronchial muscles relaxed. A different inhaled medicine is a powder that combines steroids and a bronchodilator. Inhaled corticosteroids and long-acting bronchodilators should not be used as rescue medicine.

Still another controller medicine, called a leukotriene modifier, is taken as a pill. It stops the cells in the airways from making chemicals that cause the inflammation reaction. For persons with exercise-induced asthma there are inhaled medicines called airway stabilizers which decrease hyper-sensitivity in the airways.

ALTERNATIVE THERAPIES

Alternative therapies are treatments or medicines that are not usually prescribed by a traditional medical doctor. Many believe that alternative therapies work by improving a person's overall health naturally. But, because some types of therapy can be harmful, it is absolutely essential to talk to a medical professional before beginning any alternative therapy.

Biofeedback is one type of alternative therapy for asthma and other illnesses. It uses sensitive instruments to show people how to control certain body functions. By sensing slight changes in their bodies, people can learn to influence such

Reaching Out

....

Cases of asthma are on the rise throughout the world. For more than thirty years, Americans with asthma have had access to life-saving medicines and education about their disease. Many Americans feel that it is time to share these priveleges with people in other parts of the world.

Asthma patient Dr. Paula Holmes-Eber, along with her husband and two daughters, are cycling around the world in a program called World Bike For Breath, to raise money for asthma education. In 2002 their organization donated money to open a clinic for the people of Calcutta (Kolkota), India. They helped stock the laboratory with spirometers, oximeters, nebulizers and peak flow meters to treat more than twenty thousand residents with asthma and lung disease. Another American organization, International Asthma Services, is a group of doctors and specialists who volunteer their services in asthma clinics around the world. They bring medicine, asthma camps, and education to countries such as Kenya, India, the Philippines, Nepal, Mexico, and Egypt.

things as their own heart rate or the muscles in their airways. Many hospitals have biofeedback clinics.

Another alternative therapy is massage. Massage therapy can lower stress and relax chest muscles. It can be done by a licensed massage therapist in his or her office, or sometimes at a doctor's office. Parents can learn some of the massage techniques as well.

Acupuncture is another alternative therapy that has been used to treat asthma for centuries in China. Acupuncture is becoming quite common in the United States to treat a variety of illnesses. The procedure is painless because the needles are so thin you can hardly feel them. Acupuncturists are highly trained specialists, and some medical doctors have been trained to do acupuncture as well.

Yoga is something a person can do at home to help stay healthy. Many people without asthma or any illness enjoy yoga. It is a series of rhythmic exercises and controlled breathing patterns that can stretch and relax the body, including the respiratory muscles. There are many yoga classes and videotapes available. Vitamins, herbs, and hypnosis are other forms of alternative therapies.

WARNING SIGNS

Whether a person with asthma only needs to use an inhaler once in a while, or has to take medication three to four times a day, it is important for everyone with asthma to know their asthma warning signs. After being exposed to a trigger, it may take minutes, or hours, or days for a reaction to happen. Very often, there are early warning signs that will signal when an asthma episode is on the way. A person who knows his or her early warning signs, can treat the asthma right away. Everyone's early warning signs are different. They might include a dry cough that is not from a cold, a cough that worsens at night, wheezing, an itchy throat, decreased appetite, a stomach ache, changes in sleep patterns, or feeling chilled or very hot.

There are also late warning signs that indicate the person is getting very sick. Late warning signs can include a tightness or pain in the chest, wheezing while breathing, difficulty breathing while lying down, vomiting from hard coughing, a blue gray color around the lips and eyes, fast breathing, breathing through pursed lips, tightening of the abdominal muscles, or trouble walking or talking. People with asthma should be careful if their rescue medicine does not relieve the symptoms after fifteen minutes or if he or she needs rescue medicine more than every four hours.

Action Plans

It is vital to anyone with asthma to have an action plan. The purpose of an action plan is to supply guidelines to follow if asthma symptoms develop or worsen, or in case of an emergency. The primary health care provider will help the patient develop a plan. The plan should include lists of triggers, symptoms, medications, and phone numbers of people to contact in an emergency. Copies of the action plan should be shared with emergency health care providers, family, teachers, the school nurse, bus drivers, coaches, camp counselors, dentists, and childcare providers. The patient should also carry the action plan in a wallet or backpack. Some people wear a medical alert bracelet that provides emergency information. The action plan should also be up-to-date. Each year, a primary care health provider should review the plan.

Doctors recommend that people with asthma learn to rely on a device called a **peak flow** meter. A peak flow meter measures how fast air moves out of the lungs during one quick, hard blow. The peak flow meter will give each blow a score, which the person should record on a chart or in an asthma diary. By reviewing the results in the diary, an asthma patient and his or her doctor can

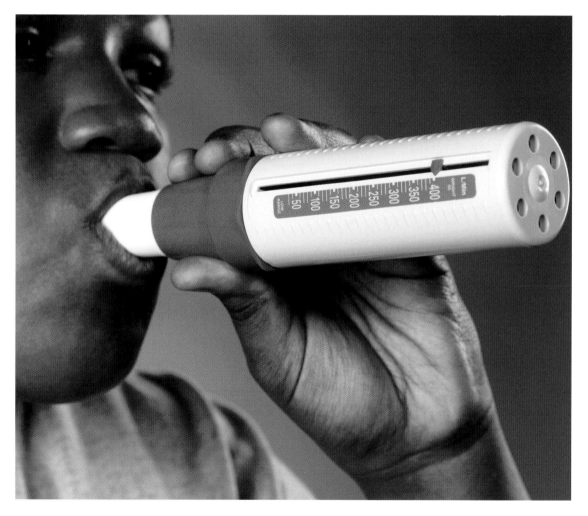

A young patient uses a peak flow meter to measure his lung function.

find out if the asthma is under control and what changes, if any need to be made in medicine. All peak flow meters work in the same general way, but each manufacturer makes its version slightly differently. A person gets the most accurate readings by always using only his or her own peak flow meter, so it is best to keep it nearby at all times.

COPING WITH ASTHMA

Along with their struggle to breathe, people with asthma also struggle to "fit in." At home, they may feel guilty that they get so much attention. At school, they may feel embarrassed to carry around inhalers and be heard wheezing and gasping. Sometimes a person with asthma feels badly about being different. He or she may feel depressed to be left out of outdoor activities, field trips, or sports. Some people with asthma say that others think they are scary when they are having an attack, or that they might spread a contagious disease. In order to fit in, some pretend they do not have the disease at all.

All of these feelings are very common and understandable. Having the support of friends, classmates, and family members makes the difference. To get their support, education about asthma is the key. The more others know about the disease the easier it is for them to accept and encourage the patient. Students with asthma should explain to their classmates that their condition is not contagious and that it can be controlled with medicine. Instead of being embarrassed about peak flow meters and inhalers,

Most people with asthma can still enjoy outdoor activities such as swimming.

students should show their classmates how these things work and what they do. When a person with asthma visits friends, he or she should show them an action plan.

Asthma is a very common childhood disease. Many students know more than one person with the disease, so no one should feel singled out. There are times when young people with asthma need to talk and share their concerns with others like them. Fortunately, there are many asthma support groups and activity-filled summer camps that are designed for their needs. It is true that people with asthma have to be more responsible about their health, but with support and teamwork, they can lead fulfilling lives. As Dr. Holmes-Eber advises, "Asthma is not an excuse for not living your life!"

Famous People with Asthma

Leonard Bernstein, composer
Coolio, singer and actor
Ludwig von Beethoven, composer
Charles Dickens, author
Martin Scorsese, film director
Bob Hope, actor and comedian
Elizabeth Taylor, actress

Amy Van Dyken, swimmer and
Olympic medalist
Jackie Joyner-Kersee, track and
field athlete and Olympic medalist
Art Monk, football player
John F. Kennedy, forty-second
president of the United States

Coolio (left), Amy Van Dyken (center), and Bob Hope (right) are just three of the millions
of people who learned to cope with asthma.

GLOSSARY

airways—Hollow tubes that carry air into and out of the lungs during breathing. Airways include the trachea, bronchi, and bronchioles.

allergen—A substance that causes an allergic reaction.

alveoli—Tiny air sacs in the lungs at the ends of the airways. Alveoli are where gases in the air are exchanged with those in the blood. The blood picks up oxygen, and releases carbon dioxide.

antibody—A protein found in blood and in tissue fluids. It attaches to foreign substances that get into the body. Antibodies are produced by B-cells (a type of white blood cell), and are a part of the immune system.

beta-agonist—The most common type of bronchodilator medication. Albuterol is a beta-agonist.

bronchi—The airways that lead from the trachea to each lung.

bronchioles—The tiny airways that lead from the bronchi into the alveoli. They are surrounded by bands of muscle and are lined with mucus-producing cells.

bronchodilator drugs—A group of drugs that widen the airways in the lungs by relaxing the muscles around bronchioles.

chronic—Lasting a long time usually for life.

corticosteroids—A group of chemicals that help to prevent or reduce inflammation. Some are hormones produced by the adrenal glands. Others are manmade drugs.

dander—Flakes of dead skin from animals.

diagnose—To determine what is making a person sick.

episode—In asthma, a period of serious symptoms, also known as an asthma attack or asthma flare.

gene—A tiny part of a cell that determines traits and characteristics of a plant or animal. Genes are inherited from a parent or parents.

histamine—A chemical released by mast cells during colds, flu, and allergic reactions. It is largely responsible for inflammation and the production of mucus.

hypersensitivity—Being especially reactive to something. The airways of people with asthma are hypersensitive to allergens, pollution, cold air, or other triggers, which causes inflammation (swelling of the airways and tightening of bronchial muscles).

immunoglobulin E (IgE)—A type of antibody that protects the body from infection. It attaches to mast cells and is present in the airways during asthma flares.

lymphocytes—White blood cells that defend the body from invading substances.

mast cell—A part of the body's immune system, found in most body tissues. Antibodies attach to mast cells to fight foreign substances, which causes the mast cells to release histamine.

mucus—A substance secreted by tissues in the body called mucus membranes. The airways are lined by mucus membrane. The mucus it produces traps inhaled foreign particles and prevents them from getting deep into the lungs.

nebulizer—A machine that mixes medicine and sterile saline fluid to form a mist which a person inhales through a mask or a mouthpiece.

peak flow—A measure of how well the respiratory system is functioning. It measures how much air a person can blow out of the lungs, and how fast.

pollen—Fine particles released by plants that often irritate the airways of people with asthma and with allergies.

pulmonary function tests (PFT)—A series of tests done to determine whether a person has breathing problems, and what those problems are.

smog—An accumulation of ground-level ozone, caused when sunlight falls on air polluted by industrial smoke and exhaust gases from vehicles.

spirometer—A machine used to measure how fast a person can blow out air, and how much air is blown.

symptoms—Signs that indicate the presence of a disease or illness.

toxic—Deadly.

trigger—Something that causes an asthma flare or causes asthma symptoms to worsen.

wheezing—Making a breathing sound that may be squeaky or whistling. Wheezes are due to air passing through narrowed airways.

Organizations

American Lung Association

61 Broadway, 6th Floor
New York, NY 10006
1-800-lungusa (1-800-586-4872)
www.lungusa.org

The American Lung Association has more than 100 offices located across the United States. By calling the number or visiting their Web site, you can find the local office near you. The site also includes free asthma information and links to other sites.

American Academy of Allergy, Asthma and Immunology (AAAAI, spoken as "Quad A-I")

555 East Wells Street
11th Floor
Milwaukee, WI 53202-3823
(414) 272-6071
www.aaaai.org

The organization's Web site provides helpful guidelines for asthma and allergies. You can also find the names and numbers of allergists near you.

Books

Baldwin, Carol. *Asthma*. Chicago, IL: Heinemann Library, 2003.

Gold, Susan Dudley. *Asthma*. Berkely Heights, NJ: Enslow Publishers, 2000.

Hyde, Margaret O. and Elizabeth H. Forsyth. *Living with Asthma*. New York: Walker, 1995.

Lennard-Brown, Sarah. *Asthma*. Austin, TX: Raintree Steck-Vaughn, 2003.

Peters, Celeste A. *Allergies, Asthma, and Exercise*. Austin, TX: Raintree Steck-Vaughn, 2000.

Simpson, Carolyn. *Coping with Asthma*. New York: Rosen Publishing Group, 1995.

Simpson, Carolyn. *Everything You Need to Know About Asthma*. New York: Rosen Publishing Group, 1998.

Strauss, Peggy Guthart. *Relieve the Squeeze: How to Take Control of Your Asthma*. New York: Viking, 2000.

Weiss, Jonathan H., PhD. *Breathe Easy: Young People's Guide to Asthma*. Washington, D.C.: American Psychological Association, 1994.

Web Sites

Asthma and Allergy Foundation of America (AAFA)
http://www.aafa.org

Asthma Facts and Statistics
(Canadian Lung Association)
http://www.lung.ca/asthma/facts.html

Asthma Tutorial
(Children's Medical Center of the University of Virginia)
http://www.people.virginia.edu/~smb4v/tutorials/asthma/asthma1.html

Asthma Wizard
(National Jewish Medical and Research Center)
http://www.njc.org/wizard/wizard.html

Everything About Asthma
(Asthma Society of Canada)
http://asthma-kids.ca/about

Just for Kids!
(U.S. Environmental Protection Agency)
http://www.epa.gov/asthma/justforkids.html

Kids' Asthma Check
(American College of Allergy, Asthma & Immunology)
http://allergy.mcg.edu/lifequality/kac2.html

KidsHealth for Kids
http://www.kidshealth.org/kid/health_problems/allergy/asthma.html

National Asthma Education and Prevention Program (NAEP) /
National Heart, Lung, and Blood Institute (NHLBI)
http://www.nhlbi.nih.gov

Playtime: Games and Activities for Kids
(Allergy & Asthma Network Mothers of Asthmatics AANMA)
http://www.aanma.org/playtime

What's Asthma All About?
http://www.whatsasthma.org

INDEX

ABOUT THE AUTHOR

Ruth Bjorklund lives on Bainbridge Island, a ferry ride from away Seattle, Washington, with her husband and two children. In researching this book, she formed a strong appreciation for the courage shown by young people with asthma and for the caring concern of their parents, friends, and health care providers.